Pascal Payen–Appenzeller

FANCY FANS

Parangon

Title page
Top:
The Warrior's Farewell, verso: *The Farmyard.* Painted vellum. Painted ivory sticks. Holland, 1700-1720.
Center:
Mourning fan. Chantilly lace on organza with appliqué painted cartouche on chicken skin. Burgau mother-of-pearl sticks with engraved lace effect. France, late 19th century.
Bottom:
Glory to the soldiers. Printed paper. Painted wood sticks. France, 1918.

Following page
Bottom:
The Triumph of Venus. Painted ivory brisé fan. Tortoiseshell sticks. France, 1890-1895.
Right:
Love at the Théâtre Français. Enamelled and gilt metal with inlaid rhinestones. France, 1870-1880.

We would like to thank the following persons for their assistance in the realization of this book: Anne Hoguet, for her generous sharing of time and knowledge; Hémylie Le Roux; Monique Prévost; Marie-Louise Roussel and Monique Morenne.

The fans presented in this book are conserved in the following collections:
Atelier Hoguet, Musée de l'éventail;
Hervé Hoguet;
Atelier Anne Hoguet.

Translation: William Wheeler
© L'Aventurine, Paris, 2000.
ISBN 2-914199-13-9

Contents

Fans throughout History

The history of the fan reflects the various itineraries which brought it to Europe, as much as it does archeological discoveries. Marco Polo and caravans brought fans back from Asia, and more specifically from China; hence, the Far East claims the invention. Museums and literature, however, have proved that Ancient Egypt was several steps ahead. There were in fact two routes, a very ancient one, and the other linked to exchanges in more modern times. The Ashmolean Museum in Oxford, England, conserves a club in its collections found in digs at Abydos, in Upper Egypt, dating probably from the third millennium B.C. It is thought to have belonged to King Scorpios. Several fans are carved on the club. The complete object had a handle and was covered with ostrich feathers or a type of palm leaves. Symbols of happiness and celestial repose, Assyrian fans were square and used to cool beverages. According to a legend from the Middle Ages, Eve broke off a tree branch to fan herself while contemplating Eden. The fifth century Indian poet and sage Valmiki wrote concerning the coronation of Rama: "We had prepared a fly whisk, a magnificent fan decorated with radiant garlands..." In *The Education of Cyrus* by Xenophon, fly whisks were associated with royalty. Combining the sacred and the practical, the first fans characterized developed societies in tropical zones. Handscreens arrived in Greece via Phrygia. They were

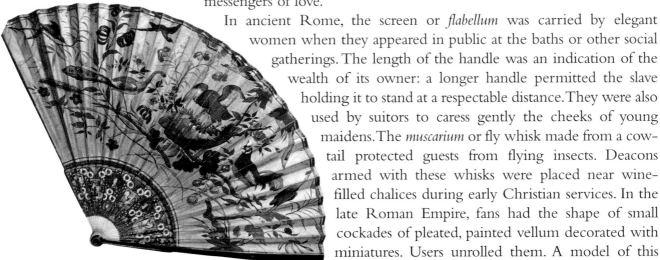

first shaped like plane leaves with a handle and were often decorated with lotus leaves or bouquets of peacock feathers, symbols of royal power. Since they were offerings to Aphrodite, they might have been considered as messengers of love.

In ancient Rome, the screen or *flabellum* was carried by elegant women when they appeared in public at the baths or other social gatherings. The length of the handle was an indication of the wealth of its owner: a longer handle permitted the slave holding it to stand at a respectable distance. They were also used by suitors to caress gently the cheeks of young maidens. The *muscarium* or fly whisk made from a cowtail protected guests from flying insects. Deacons armed with these whisks were placed near winefilled chalices during early Christian services. In the late Roman Empire, fans had the shape of small cockades of pleated, painted vellum decorated with miniatures. Users unrolled them. A model of this type of fan conserved in the Bargello Museum in Florence, Italy, is forty-five centimeters in diameter. Used at the Abbey of Tournus, France, it probably dates from the ninth century.

Previous to Vatican II, two large feather fans preceded the *Sedia Gestatoria* in papal ceremonies, thus continuing a tradition dating from the time of the pharaohs. The history of fans was progressively to take a new turn with a change of names and a technical revolution. They would become indispensable accessories for men as well as women and, contrary to general opinion, their use was uninterrupted throughout history. In France, fans were always present at the royal court. In the twelfth century, a cockade cooled Louis VII's feverish brow on his sick bed. Precious materials were used for these fashion accessories. Clemence of Hungary, wife of Louis X, had an embroidered silk fan; the handle of Jeanne d'Evreux's model was in ivory and jet; Charles V had a round fan with an ebony handle. Handscreens with gilt silver handles were also fashionable. In 1384, a new word appeared in French for fan, *esventour,* borrowed from southern dialects, showing its links with hot climates.

Upon return from his first voyage to the Americas in 1493, Christopher Columbus presented a feather fan to Queen Isabella. Spanish and Portuguese merchants introduced pleated folding fans, a Japanese invention, in Europe. They had been adopted by the Chinese and it was the sixteenth century Portuguese colonists living there who discovered them.

Flora and Fauna. Painted leather on paper. Ivory and tortoiseshell sticks. France, early 18th century.

Bergerie. Painted and embroidered silk with sequins. Engraved and gilt ivory sticks. France, 1770.

Ribbons. Painted textured paper. Pierced, engraved and gilt ivory sticks. Europe, 1740-1745.

They arrived in France, via Italy, during the reign of the Valois kings. Different models coexisted in the two countries; although feather fans were the most prevalent, there was also flag fans (Veronese painted some models), parchment or silk leaf fans, *brisé* fans, "leafless" fans consisting of sticks and guards held together only by a ribbon at their summit. Eight-stick pleated folding fans opened 45°, 90° or 360°, in a cockade. Precious information concerning fan models can be gleaned from fan source books published in France and England. The present French word for fan *éventail* entered literature through Brantôme's *Vies des dames galantes* published in 1665.

Fans in sixteenth century France, during the reigns of Catherine de Medici and her son Henri III, were worn at the waist attached to a gold chain. Two pieces conserved in the collections of the Renaissance Museum in Ecouen, France, illustrate why fans were considered like jewels. Inlaid mica chips acting as small mirrors sparkle, especially when the fans are fluttered. Imitating highly fashionable reticulate lace also used for fans, cutouts of the vellum leaf on one of them permits mask play. At that time, Italy was an important European center of fan production. During the seventeenth century, French artists Jacques Callot and Abraham Bosse would define the canons of painted leaves: Callot preferred a single scene occupying the entire space, whereas Bosse advocated three smaller cartouches. Coincd as "screens of modesty" or "useful Zephyr" in the affected jargon of the *Précieuses* at the court of Louis

Pierced, engraved and gilt-leaf white mother-of-pearl monture. France, 19th century.

XIV, fans accompanied courtiers all year long, although they were not used at Versailles as spanking rods for children as was the practice in England at the court of Elisabeth I.

The Sun King created the fan makers guild and mastership by letters patent dated January 15 and February 15, 1678. Most fanmakers grouped in Paris on the rue Saint-Denis. *Montures,* the fan framework, remained the exclusive domain of *tabletiers* and *peigniers* (comb makers). France pro-

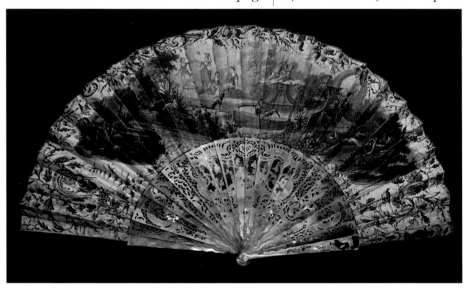

Venitian Feast, verso. Painted vellum. Pierced, gilt-leaf ivory sticks. France, *ca.* 1750.

gressively became the leading center of production for Europe. Even typically Chinese brisé fans were manufactured in Parisian workshops.

Classical mythology dominated subject matter and contemporary princesses were represented as goddesses draped in flowing robes. Besides the symbolism of the images, a code language of the fan developed, imported from austere Spain where it was used by lovers to circumvent the strict moral code imposed by the Catholic Church.

The reputation of French-produced fans grew throughout the eighteenth century (models with French subjects were produced in China). Borrowed from cabinet and furniture makers, the *vernis Martin*, a lengthy varnishing technique protected painted *brisé* fan sticks. Mother of pearl with its rainbow colors was introduced into fan making. Pierced gilt sticks with low relief carved medallions were also frequently decorated with miniatures. Celebrated artists the likes of Watteau and Boucher while greatly influencing fan subject matter, were not however encouraged to paint leaves themselves as fan makers preferred jealously to guard their monopoly.

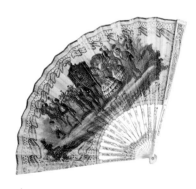

The Pedlar. Chromolithography on paper. Ivory sticks. Spain, 1810-1820.

Secret fans flourished late in the century at a time when simplicity was in fashion. The rapidly evolving current events of Revolutionary times provided fans with a new role as highly visible tracts. Twenty-two stick models were reduced to sixteen or fourteen. Common paper and wood replaced more precious materials.

Fans went out of favor, at least in France, in the first decades of the nineteenth century, although Europeans were at a lack for a replacement. The

Views of Rome. Painted chicken skin. Engraved ivory sticks. Italy, 1770-1775.

invention of watercolor by the Englishman John Robert Cousins would give new life to this art form. In the meantime, sequins during the reign of Marie-Antoinette and diamond-covered guards on imperial models continued the tradition of fans as sparkling fashion accessories.

The Great Exhibitions, the elegant luxury of the Second Empire exemplified by the Spanish culture of Eugenie of Montijo, wife of Napoleon III, and the opening of covered arcades in Paris making it an ideal place for fashionable strolling: all these events invigorated the fan business. Impressionism made itself known to a widening audience through fans and amateur watercolorists of polite society occupied themselves with leaf painting. World War I dealt a serious blow to the profession and, in France, it remained inactive until the creation of the Fan Museum on the premises of the Atelier Hoguet in 1993. At the same time the numerous fans sold in public auctions proved the growing interest of collectors in the field.

Fans on haute couture catwalks and in cabaret revues are proof that fans still have a role to play and that they will once again accompany fashionable women as they stroll on the Champs-Elysées.

Comité des fêtes de Mulhouse. Printed paper. Wood sticks. Chambrelent, Paris, 1922.

Fan Craftsmen

Fan making requires the skills of numerous craftsmen: the *tabletier* prepared the *monture* or framework, one or several artists painted the leaf, the fan makers pleated the leaf before mounting it on the framework. Sticks and guards were first roughly cut out with a saw. Different types of tools were used depending on the nature of the raw materials. Sticks were formed and filed to give them their final shape. They were then scraped to erase tool marks. Ivory, bone and mother of pearl were polished with a stiff brush and linseed oil; polishing paste was used on horn and sandpaper on wood. The sticks were ready to be pierced. This technique, like engraving and sculpture using burins and chisels, required the sharp eyes and steady hands of young workers – in the nineteenth century models were often copied, and youth and good health counted more than experience. Thousands of microscopic holes had to be pierced for certain motifs. The gilder applied gold leaf with a wire burnishing brush. In the nineteenth century, less expensive gold powder applied with a brush was also used. Folding and *brisé* fans both require a rivet at the bottom of the guard sticks allowing the fan to open and close without falling apart. Rivets were often decorated with real or imitation jewels.

For leather (sturdy vellum or more finely treated skin, called "chicken skin"), cloth or paper leaves, the pattern corresponded to the dimensions of the fan. The leaf was painted and decorated before it was pleated. Until 1770, pleating was done by hand with its imperfections and irregularities. At that date, the Frenchman Martin Petit developed a mold consisting of two sheets of cardboard divided in about fifteen parts. Seventy years later, his descendant Jean-Edouard Petit improved the divider and developed a series of ninety molds numbered from sixty to one hundred fifty. Mold No. 90, for example, produced a *monture* of sixteen inches and sixteen sticks. Developed at the French Revolution, the metrical system was curiously never adopted by the Petits, nor fan

Blond tortoiseshell with rhinestone monogram. France, 1880.

10

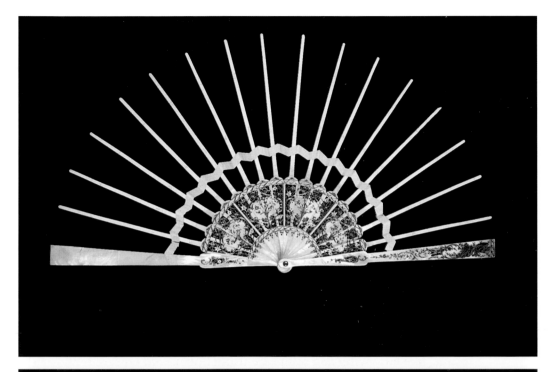

Pierced, engraved and gilt-leafed white mother-of-pearl montures. Top, by Marius Hoguet. Bottom, by Joseph Hoguet. France, 1890.

makers in general. Generalized use of cloth leaves facilitated the use of molds. Final decorative touches were added before the pleated leaf was attached to the monture. The sticks were joined one by one to the leaf. A simple model could be mounted in about ten minutes. Afterwards, the leaf was edged or bordered in a manner depending on its style and material. The final touch was a silk cord, or tassel attached to the loop below the rivet. Before the fan left the studio, it was thoroughly checked for imperfections.

Nowadays, most of these specialized crafts have practically disappeared as present-day fan production is very limited. Today the work is divided between the *tabletier* for the *monture* and the artist who creates and decorates the leaf. There is new interest on the part of contemporary artists for fan painting as there is on the part of art collectors to acquire these works.

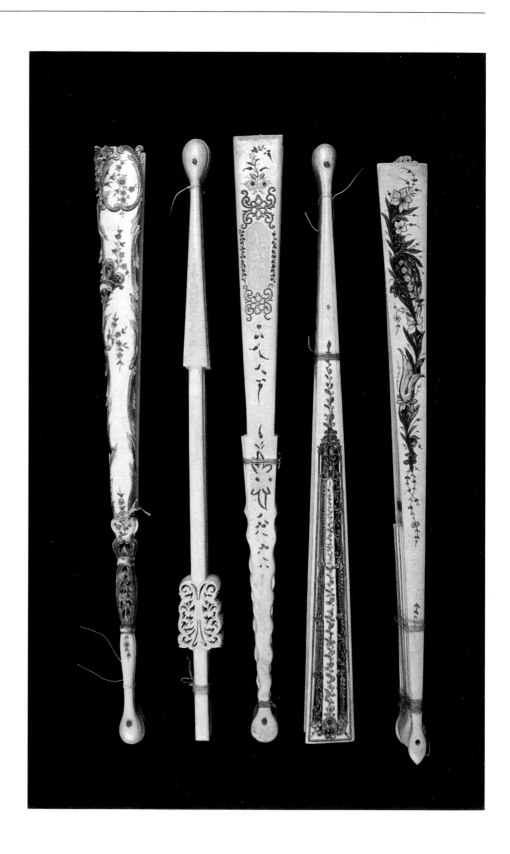

Decorated ivory and bone
montures. France,
1880–1890.

Blond horn monture with inlaid mother of pearl. France, 1905–1910.

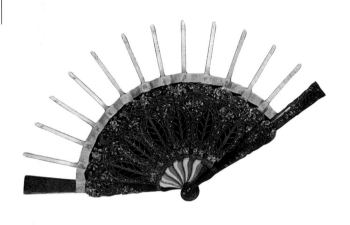

Pierced, engraved and gilt ivory monture. France, 1880–1885.

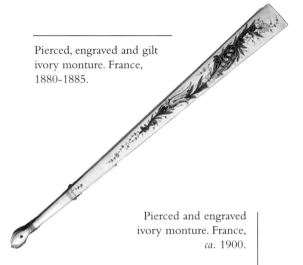

Pierced and engraved ivory monture. France, *ca.* 1900.

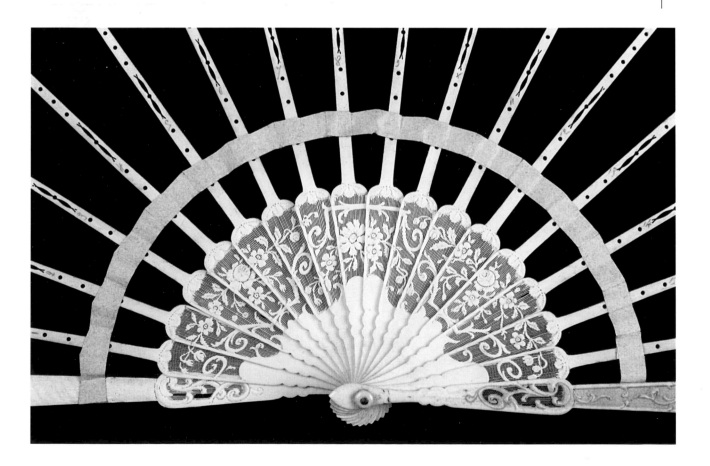

Folding Paintings

Fan leaves were signed by artists starting in the 1870's. The Fan section of the French Society of Watercolorists attracted crowds and insured the success of their annual *Salons*. The Goncourt brothers' writings on Watteau made him an ever-present model for painters. Soldé presented his *Hommage à Watteau* around 1860. This gifted artist collaborated with two well-known fan houses, Meyer and Alexandre. Fan painting was however a traditionally female domain. Louise Abbema, Rosa Bonheur and Madeleine Lemaire were recognized artists working regularly as leaf painters. Other notable artists in the field from the pre-Impressionist period included the Louis brothers, Maurice Leloir, Eugène Lami and Edouard Detaille. In paintings, fans seemed ubiquitous, for example in Edouard Manet's, *Nina de Callias* (1873). Japanese screens line the bedroom wall behind the reclining woman. The themes of woman and exoticism, plus a decided concern for modernity, led an Edouard Degas, fascinated by page setting and centring, directly to fan painting. The half circle dimensions of the leaf obliged the artist to create a dynamic balance. At the fourth Impressionist exhibition held in 1879 Degas presented five leaves and Pissarro twelve. Their talents as colorists and their penchant for asymmetry designated them as natural fan painters. Pissarro, in fact, lived off his fan painting, leaving at his death more than eigthy models. Gauguin, however, also painted leaves but was incapable of selling even one. His fan *Arearea* now hangs in the Houston Museum of Fine Art. Inspired by the painting of the same name in the Orsay Museum in Paris, it is a concert of highly colorful harmonies bringing to mind a Golden Age reflected through Tahitian landscapes. Gauguin brought a magic to his fans which his contemporaries could not fathom. It was only after fans had lost their moment of glory that Gauguin's fans and his artistic work were justly appreciated. The whole Impressionist school and the Nabis as well, used fan painting as exercise drills. The painter of idealized romance, Maurice Denis, could not ignore this symbol of love. Unfortunately, many of the leaves painted by artists were never mounted as fans, for they lacked the necessary contacts to sell them to fan houses. Many were simply distributed to friends as gifts.

After paintings by Greuze.
Printed paper. Wood sticks.
France, 1925.

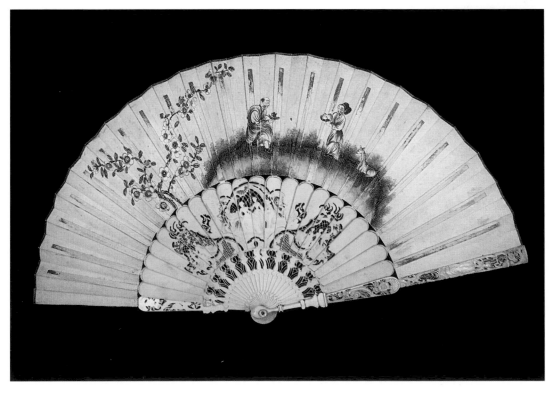

Offering of fruit. Recto and verso. Painted vellum. Painted and engraved ivory sticks. England or Holland, 1750–1760.

Mythology

Classical mythology was a principal source of inspiration for seventeenth and eighteenth century artists and crafts-men, clearly defining the fan in its cultural context. As an instrument of royal power, myths were often employed to illustrate historical events. Crowded battle scenes and royal audiences both benefitted from the folding and unfolding fan, as did the division of the leaf surface into several secondary scenes like on a wide theater stage. Imposing forms such as horses posed the problem of continuing figures over several folds, as did long dresses and ceremonial court robes, but they also allowed artists to show off their specific talents as fan painters. The most dramatic scenes of the repertoire were often borrowed from Homer or from other ancient source material. Agamemnon encounters Iphigenia; Jason takes posssession of the Golden Fleece: mythological subjects such as these led to *Thétis surrending her weapons to Achilles,* still considered a commercial subject as late as 1770. Large central scenes were replaced by appliqué gouache cartouches placed in the center of the leaf. Venus, Selene and Psyche compete for attention. The sea nymphs on a 1900 fan were painted in gouache on a leather leaf, the sculpted ivory sticks were treated as seaweed-covered coral branches. Women, nature and fantasy had definitively triumphed over sacred ancient imagery.

Rinaldo in the garden of Armida. Recto and verso. Painted chicken skin on paper. Pierced, engraved and gilt-leaf marbled tortoiseshell sticks with low relief carving. France 1750-1760.

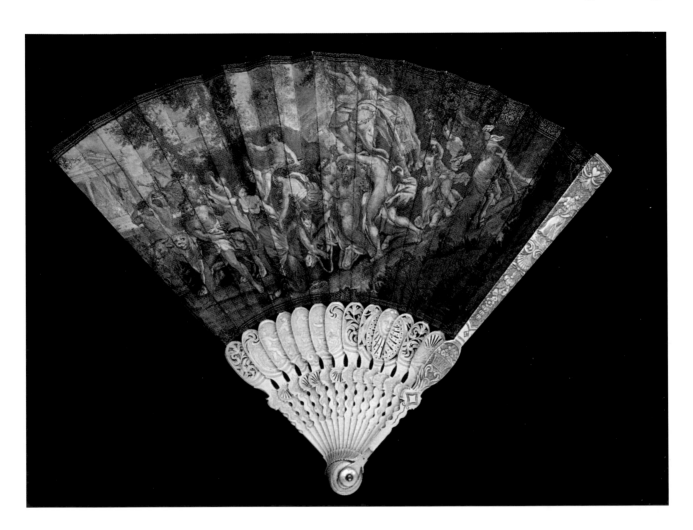

Bacchanalia. Painted vellum.
Pierced and engraved ivory
sticks with inlaid mother of
pearl. Chinese *monture* and
French leaf. 1740–1745.

The Birth of Venus. Brisé
fan. Painted ivory with
inlaid mother of pearl.
France, 1720–1725.

The Death of Dido. Painted
chicken skin. Engraved
ivory sticks with mother
of pearl. France,
1730–1740.

The Embarcation of Helen. Painted
leather. Pierced, engraved and gilt
ivory sticks. France, 1745-1750.

The Triumph of Venus.
Painted vellum. Ivory
sticks and inlaid mother-
of-pearl guards. France,
1730–1740.

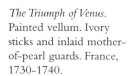

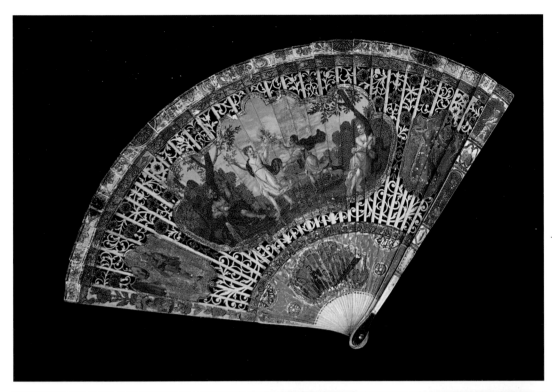

Apollon and Daphne.
Painted ivory and
tortoiseshell *brisé* fan.
Painted chicken skin
ribbon. France,
1710-1720.

Country scene, verso of
Triumph of Cupid. Painted
ivory *brisé* fan. France,
1720-1725.

The Return of the Warrior.
Painted chicken skin.
Engraved ivory sticks.
France, 1720–1730.

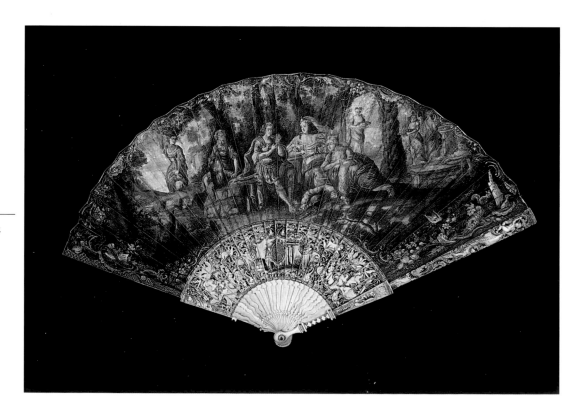

The Repose of the Warrior.
Painted chicken skin.
Painted and engraved
ivory sicks. France,
1740–1745.

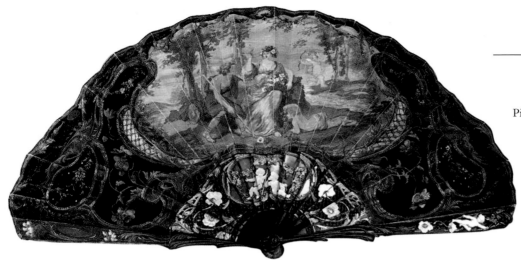

Flora and the Shepherd.
Painted paper and
embroidered organza.
Pierced, engraved and gilt
tortoiseshell sticks with
inlaid mother of pearl.
France, 1895–1900.

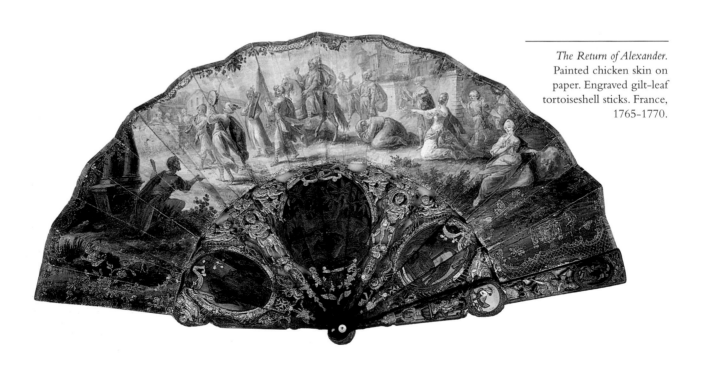

The Return of Alexander.
Painted chicken skin on
paper. Engraved gilt-leaf
tortoiseshell sticks. France,
1765–1770.

The Bible

Changes in fan styles accompanied the evolution of society. Biblical subjects were all the rage in seventeenth century France as they were in eighteenth century Russia. This country regularly adopted French models after a fashion. The theme however was not an exclusive one. It corresponded to a Christian society enraptured with Antiquity and mythology. On fans with both sides decorated, the reverse, or inner side, was covered with a floral motif, while Old Testament stories were reserved for the noble side, facing outward towards society. Some books and characters regularly inspired artists: Abraham in Genesis, Moses and his wife Cippora in Exodus, Saul, David and his wife Abigail in Samuel. The crowning of Esther in the book by the same name is the archetypical figure generally associated with marriage. Biblical-themed fans usually illustrate fortuitous encounters whereas subjects from Antiquity are more dramatic in nature, sacrifices alternate with battles and scenes of royal justice.

Moses beating the rock. Painted vellum. Ivory sticks. England, 1700–1710.

Saul and David, verso. Painted kid. Painted gilt–leaf white mother–of–pearl sticks. 1740–1750.

The Flight to Egypt. Painted vellum. Pierced and engraved ivory sticks. England, 1745–1750.

The Sacrifice of Abraham. Painted chicken skin on paper. Engraved ivory sticks with inlaid mother of pearl. Chinese *monture* and Italian leaf, 1740–1745.

Jacob and Rachel. Painted monochrome vellum. Engraved white mother-of-pearl sticks. Holland, 1760–1770.

Genre scenes

The century of Louis XV begins in 1750. This apparently odd chronology actually applies rather accurately to our impression of it, that is to say, pastoral scenes called *bergerades* (from *berger*, shepherd) which take over fans until Marie-Antoinette imposed a rustic style. A shepherd or a marquis, depending on the situation, talks amorously with his lady friend while cherubs fly around a flower-laden altar. Antoine Watteau and Jean-Honoré Fragonard among others inspired innumerable images painted for fans, occasionally of very mediocre quality. The ever-growing number of provincial art salons gave birth to a new type of folk art. Spirited revelling or elegant dinners, country fairs and amusement parks, hunting and other outdoor activities make up the repertoire of fans during this hundred year period with its increasingly bourgeois aspirations. The nineteenth century would repeat these themes time and time again. Venus, the goddesss of Love, is figured in a medallion on certain precious *montures* according her high patronage to love in a pastoral scene illustrated above on the leaf.

Amusement in a park. Painted chicken skin on paper. Gilt-leaf ivory sticks with inlaid mother of pearl. France, 1760–1770.

The Luncheon. Chromolithography on paper. Pierced, engraved and gilt-leaf bone sticks with inlaid mother of pearl. France 1855–1860.

Wine Fest. Painted ivory *brisé* fan. France or Holland, 1690.

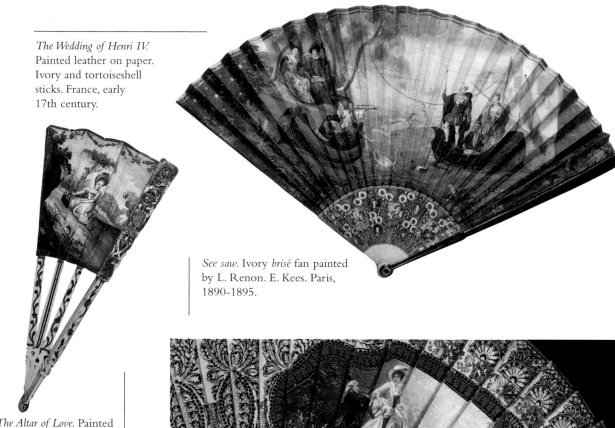

The Wedding of Henri IV. Painted leather on paper. Ivory and tortoiseshell sticks. France, early 17th century.

The Altar of Love. Painted paper. Engraved gilt-leaf ivory sticks. France, 1770-1780.

See saw. Ivory *brisé* fan painted by L. Renon. E. Kees. Paris, 1890–1895.

Following page:
The Coronation. Painted chicken skin. Pierced, engraved and gilt-leaf ivory sticks. Europe, 1745-1750.

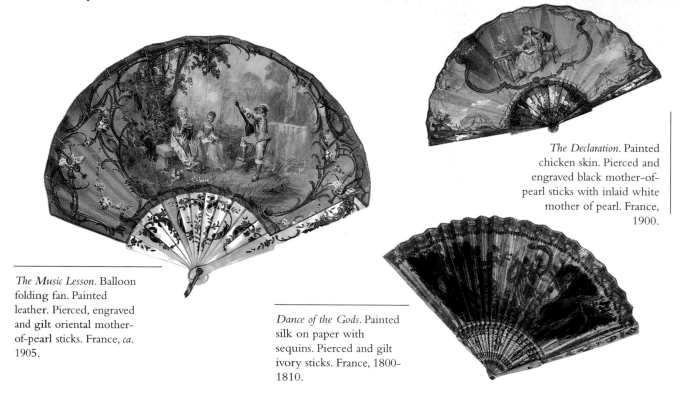

The Declaration. Painted chicken skin. Pierced and engraved black mother-of-pearl sticks with inlaid white mother of pearl. France, 1900.

The Music Lesson. Balloon folding fan. Painted leather. Pierced, engraved and **gilt** oriental mother-of-pearl sticks. France, *ca.* 1905.

Dance of the Gods. Painted silk on paper with sequins. Pierced and gilt ivory sticks. France, 1800-1810.

The Lesson. Painted silk palmette fan. Engraved and **painted** ivory sticks with inlaid burgau mother of pearl. France, *ca.* 1860.

Following page:
The Hunt. Recto and verso. Chromolithography on paper. Engraved white mother-of-pearl sticks. France, 1840-1850.

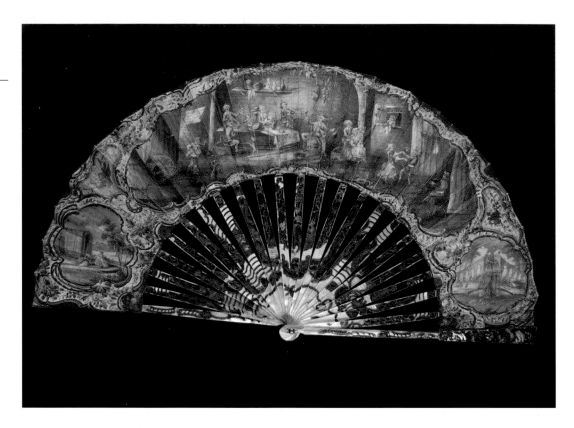

The Inn. Painted chicken skin. Engraved white mother-of-pearl sticks. Holland, 1760-1770.

An Afternoon in Society. Paint and chromolithigraphy on chicken skin. Pierced, engraved and bronze-gilt burgau mother-of-pearl sticks. France, 1840-1850.

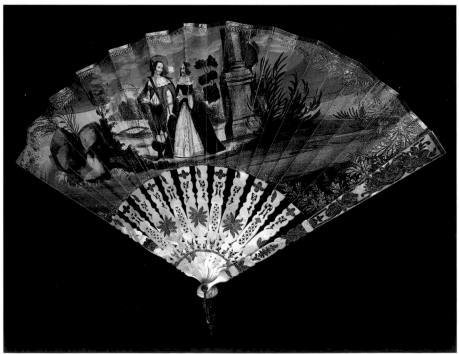

Scène galante. Painted ivory brisé fan. Painted bone sticks. France, 1860.

The Union. Painted vellum. Engraved ivory sticks. Holland or England, 1750–1760.

The Dance. Painted chicken skin. Pierced and engraved ivory sticks with inlaid white mother of pearl. France or Italy, 1720–1730.

Pastoral Life. Painted chicken skin on paper. Engraved, gilt and painted ivory sticks. France, 1750–1755.

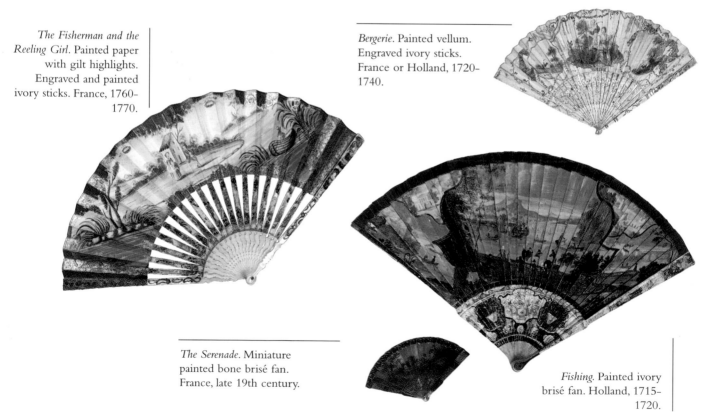

The Fisherman and the Reeling Girl. Painted paper with gilt highlights. Engraved and painted ivory sticks. France, 1760–1770.

Bergerie. Painted vellum. Engraved ivory sticks. France or Holland, 1720–1740.

The Serenade. Miniature painted bone brisé fan. France, late 19th century.

Fishing. Painted ivory brisé fan. Holland, 1715–1720.

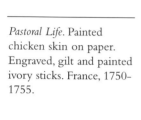

Wine harvest. Painted chicken skin. Pierced, engraved and painted ivory sticks. France, 1745–1750.

Pastoral Scene. Bone brisé fan painted by Mrs Friedmann, 1940–1960. Monture by E. Kees. Paris, 1900.

Exotic Fans

Fascinated by its colonies, by Russia and its Byzantine culture, and by folklore in general, nineteenth century Europe was beguiled by exoticism. In France, the adventure novels by the marine officer Pierre Loti played an influential role from their date of publication in the 1870's until the 1920's. The taste for Orientalism and more specifically Japonism encouraged artists and craftsmen to propose models which reflected these tendencies in their subjects and manufacturing techniques. Japonism exemplified the decade 1875-1885, which became a decorative style based largely on floral motifs of irises, roses and mock orange. Orientalism enjoyed its moment of glory in the 1910's. A very eclectic movement, it principally influenced fashion and current events. The ever-popular Thousand and One Nights inspired the most diverse compositions, from the most simple to the most luxurious. Painted or printed on paper, tulle or leather, the leaf was often given a balloon shape. Montures were rarely made from precious materials - most were in natural or stained wood; sometimes ebony was used. Wicker fans were also standard items. Their originality combined lightweight materials and simple refinement.

Ladies carried fans on their train voyages and sojourns at seaside resorts. In its insatiable taste for fans, the West copied the East where they were ubiquitous, serving all purposes in all occasions. The army seemed to remain the only fanless haven. In the East, however, a commentator marvelled: "Soldiers handle fans while under enemy fire with incredible calmness".

Paper lace on gauze. Bamboo sticks. Indochina, 1910.

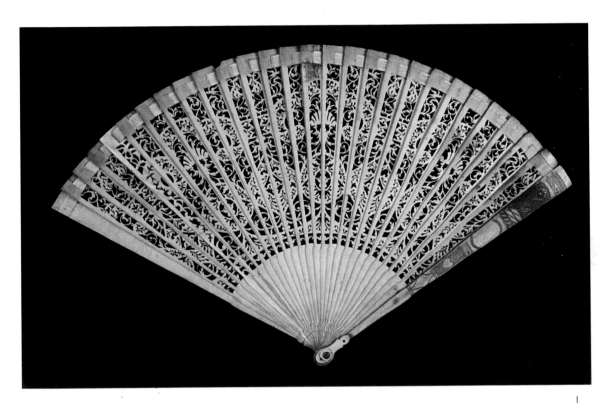

Pierced ivory brisé fan.
China, *ca.* 1710.

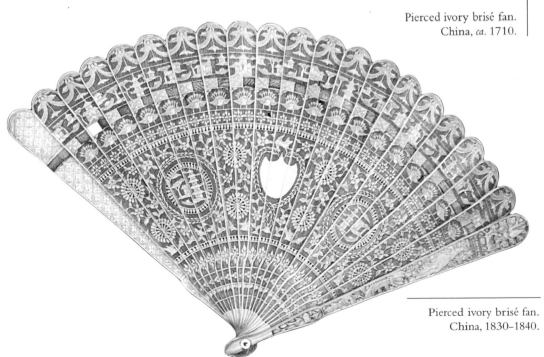

Pierced ivory brisé fan.
China, 1830–1840.

Tea Ceremony. Painted paper with inlaid burgau mother of pearl and sequins. Lacquered bamboo and ivory sticks. China, n.d.

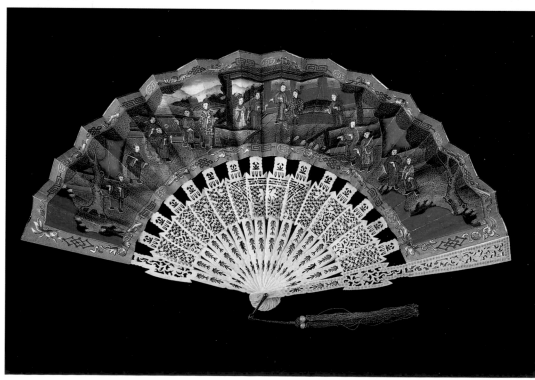

Chinese pavilions. Painted paper with collage. Pierced ivory sticks. Canton, China, 1850-1860.

China Red. Recto, verso
and guards.
Chromolithography and
paint on paper. Painted and
bronze-gilt bone sticks
with inlaid steel sequins.
France, 1850–1855.

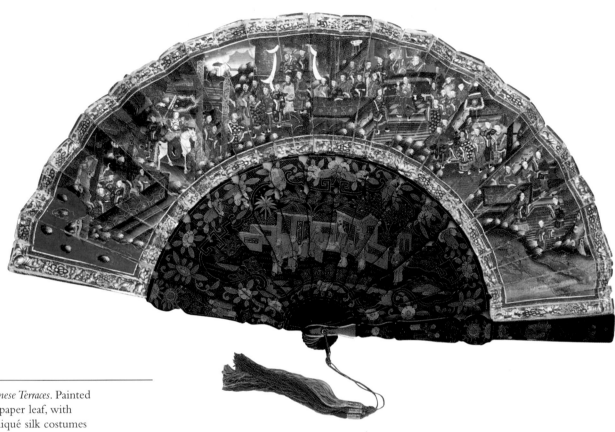

Chinese Terraces. Painted ricepaper leaf, with appliqué silk costumes and inlaid painted ivory heads. Lacquered gilt-leaf wood sticks. Canton, China, 1850–1860.

Painted silk handscreen.
Bamboo and ivory handle. Korea, late 19th century.

Painted silk handscreen, recto and verso, with appliqué silk and collage. Lacquered wood handle. Japan, late 19th century.

40

Printed silk handscreen.
Lacquered wood handle.
China, 19th century.

Pierced and gilt buffalo
skin handscreens. Buffalo
horn handle. Indonesia,
2nd half of 20th century.

Painted goose feather handscreens. Bamboo handles. China, 2nd half of 20th century.

Paper fan. Painted wood. Southern Asia, 2nd half of 20th century.

Paper fan. Painted wood. Southern Asia, 2nd half of 20th century.

43

Dried and painted leaf handscreen. Southern India, 2nd half of 20th century.

Woven and dyed raffia handscreens. Haiti, 2nd half of 20th century.

Top: Woven and dyed raffia flag screen. Libya, 2nd half of 20th century.
Bottom: Dyed straw handscreen. Tunisia. 2nd half of 20th century.

Raffia cockade. India, 2nd half of 20th century.

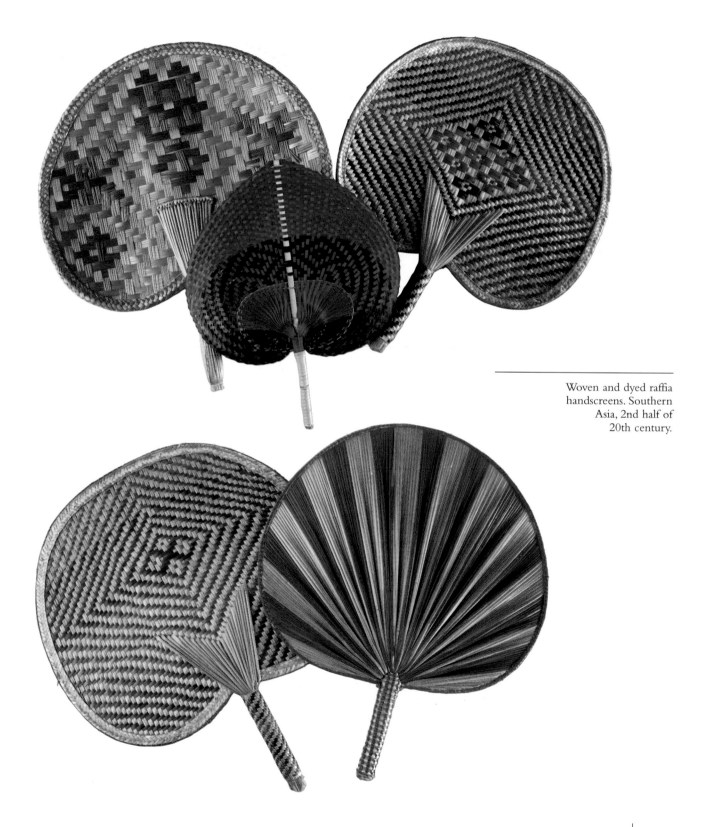

Woven and dyed raffia
handscreens. Southern
Asia, 2nd half of
20th century.

45

A Fan for Every Occasion

A fan for every occasion of daily life was a reality for the Western bourgeoisie and prominent families in the colonial empires for a short time around the turn of the twentieth century. The fan was then considered as a decorative object. Present at all ceremonies – births, marriages and funerals, fans were given at year end festivities, birthdays, family gatherings, commemorations, etc. Women arrived with a fan in their hands at banquets, masked balls and festivities of all sorts. If the playwrights Robert de Flers and Armand de Caillavet named one of their comedies *The Fan*, it was because they exemplified a society which expressed itself through these multi-purpose objects. The silversmith Christofle was once commissioned by an Indian prince to execute a musical bed at the four corners of which stood silver statues of women which, when activated, slowly moved a pharaonic fan. Civilisations were brought together by the fan, at a time when eclecticism was enthusiastically embraced.

Wedding fan. Honiton lace and painted organza. Gilt ivory sticks. France, 1890.

Wedding fan. Bead embroidered and sequins on organza gauze. Pierced white mother-of-pearl sticks. France, 1905-1910.

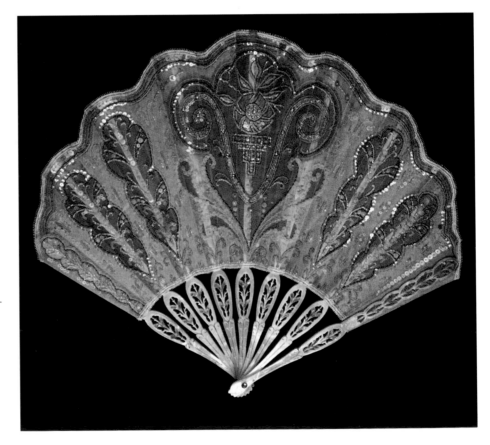

Sorrow and Fidelity. Chromolithography and paint on chicken skin on paper. Pierced ivory sticks. France, 1810–1820.

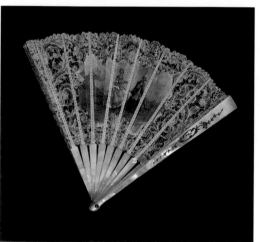

Left:
Scène galante. Painted silk on duchesse lace. Engraved and gilt white mother-of-pearl sticks. France, 1900.
Right:
Wedding fan. Painted silk with appliqué Calais lace. Bone sticks. France, 1880–1885.

Carriage of Angels. Painted silk crêpe with appliqué Venitian lace. Pierced, engraved and bronze-gilt mother-of-pearl sticks. France, 1880–1890.

Mourning fan. Painted silk. Tortoiseshell sticks. France, 1890–1900.

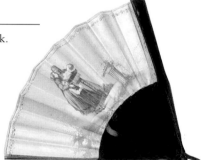

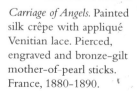

The Symbolist period announced a change in subject matter. The everlasting theme *Conversation in a garden* finally lost out to personifications of femininity. Before the *belle-époque*, fans were primarily reserved for offical ceremonies and receptions. The Great Exhibitions were perfect occasions for fan makers to introduce models corresponding to specific moments of feminine life: morning walks, afternoon dances, etc. Some were discreet accessories to complete equally reserved outfits, whereas others were conspicuously precious, capable of attracting attention at the Opera. Hostesses had guests sign a fan instead of a visitors' book. They served as masks at costume balls. The craze was such that fans became multi-purpose objects: they serve as logos, greeting cards; contests were organized with prizes for the best amateur fan maker. An article in a 1903 issue of *Femina* provided a classication for fans: "resigned" for the young lady with no dance partner, to be placed on the knees; "shrew" for the woman with something to hide, and "polite" to conceal yawns of boredom. Young debutants used them to hide behind when they blushed or let them drop to be retrieved by a prospective suitor. If they married, the mother-of-pearl and gauze fan he would buy his bride for the wedding would cost six or seven times more than the one that originally brought them together.

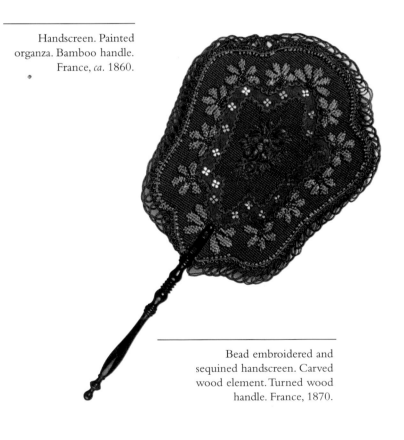

Handscreen. Painted organza. Bamboo handle. France, *ca.* 1860.

Bead embroidered and sequined handscreen. Carved wood element. Turned wood handle. France, 1870.

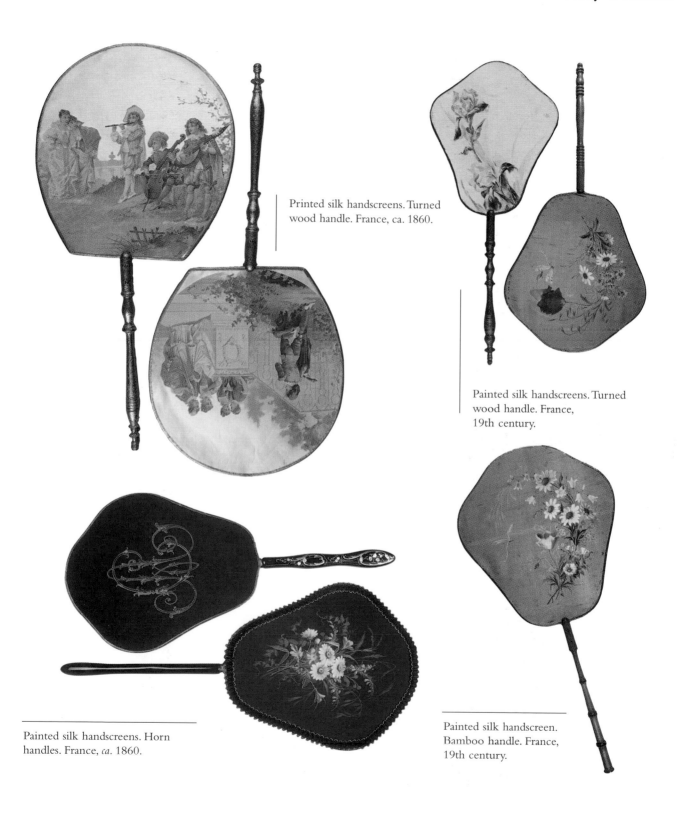

Printed silk handscreens. Turned
wood handle. France, ca. 1860.

Painted silk handscreens. Turned
wood handle. France,
19th century.

Painted silk handscreens. Horn
handles. France, *ca.* 1860.

Painted silk handscreen.
Bamboo handle. France,
19th century.

Duo. Painted and embroidered silk on chicken skin. Engraved, painted and gilt-leaf ivory sticks. France, 1770–1780.

Chantecler. Painted gauze with sequins. Painted wood sticks. France, *ca.* 1910.

Iris. Painted tarlatan. Painted Brazilian rosewood sticks. France, 1920.

Carnations. Painted organza. Blond horn sticks. France, 1920–1925.

Violets. Pierced and painted wood *brisé* fan. France, 1880.

Garden scene. Pierced and painted blond horn. Silk ribbon. France, 1815–1820.

Painted wood *brisé* fan. France, 1920–1925.

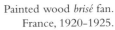

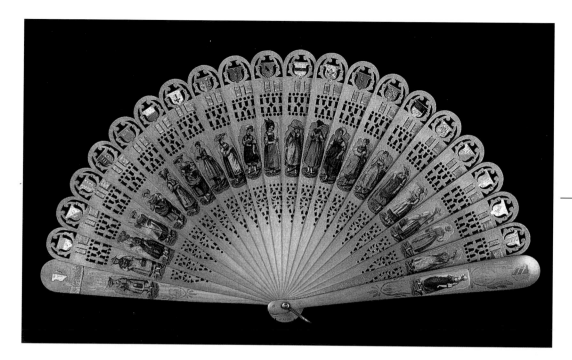

The Twenty-two Cantons. Pierced wood *brisé* fan with decals. Switzerland, 1880.

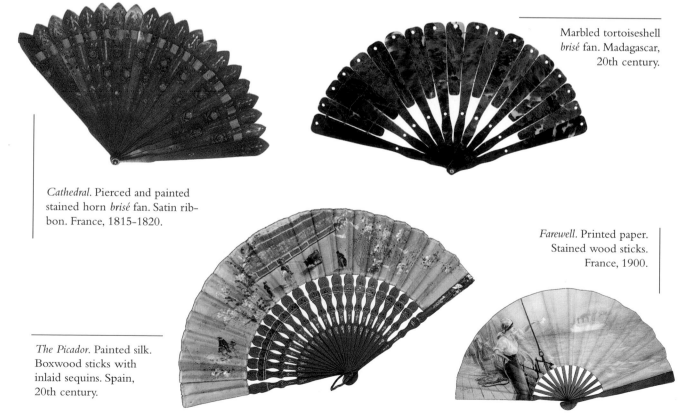

Marbled tortoiseshell *brisé* fan. Madagascar, 20th century.

Cathedral. Pierced and painted stained horn *brisé* fan. Satin ribbon. France, 1815-1820.

Farewell. Printed paper. Stained wood sticks. France, 1900.

The Picador. Painted silk. Boxwood sticks with inlaid sequins. Spain, 20th century.

Embroidered organza balloon fan with sequins. Burgau mother-of-pearl sticks with inlaid sequins. France, 1905–1910.

Embroidered organza with sequins. Stained burgau mother-of-pearl sticks. France, 1905–1910.

Embroidered and sequined silk collapsible fan . White mother-of-pearl sticks with inlaid sequins. France, 1880–1885.

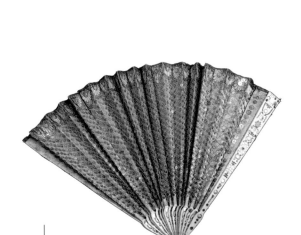

Empire. Embroidered and sequined silk with silk thread. Bone sticks with inlaid steel sequins. France, 1805–1810.

Embroidered silk and organza with sequins. Engraved and painted blond horn sticks. France, 1890–1900.

Embroidered and sequined gauze. Pierced mother-of-pearl sticks with inlaid sequins and studs. France, 1805–1810.

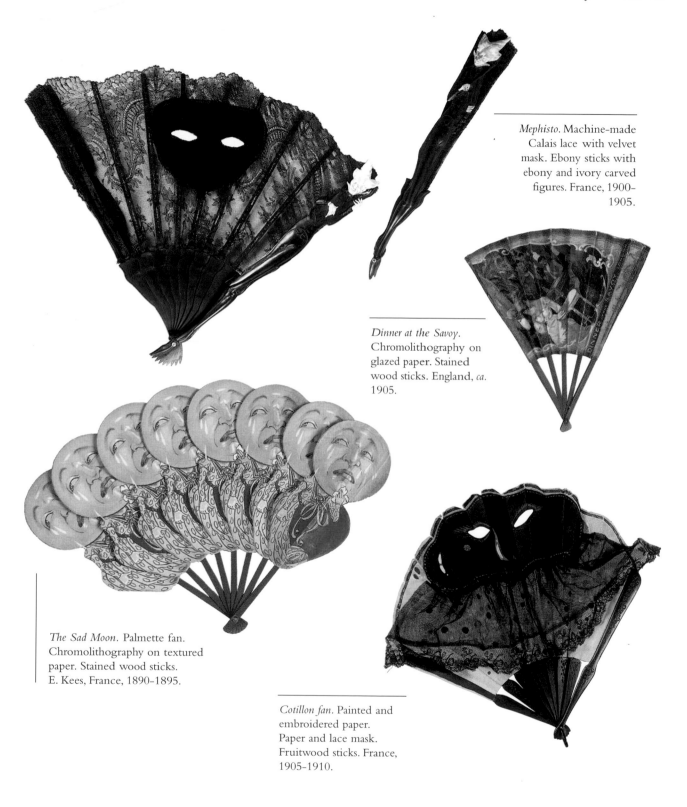

Mephisto. Machine-made Calais lace with velvet mask. Ebony sticks with ebony and ivory carved figures. France, 1900–1905.

Dinner at the Savoy. Chromolithography on glazed paper. Stained wood sticks. England, *ca.* 1905.

The Sad Moon. Palmette fan. Chromolithography on textured paper. Stained wood sticks. E. Kees, France, 1890–1895.

Cotillon fan. Painted and embroidered paper. Paper and lace mask. Fruitwood sticks. France, 1905–1910.

Feather fans

Long used for handscreens, feathers staged a comeback in the 1860's when they were used on folding fans. South Africa furnished European markets with domesticated ostrich feathers. Six wholesale auctions were held each year in London where fan makers procured the three different qualities of feathers. Top quality white feathers came from the extremities of the wings and the rump of male birds. Intermediate quality grey and brown speckled "femina" feathers came from females. The rest of the feathers were dyed black or fashionable, sometimes extremely bright colors. These were directly attached to the fan sticks or mixed with domestic barnyard feathers. Used mostly for formal occasions, *belle-époque* feather fans were costly; thus, it was not unusual for a hunter to offer their feathered hunting trophies to the woman of his heart to be transformed into a fan. Some large fans required up to five hundred feathers and an adult jay had only twelve usable feathers!

Dyed Chinese cock feather fan. Galalith sticks. Paris, 1910.

Dyed Chinese cock feather fan, (opened and closed). Galalith sticks. Paris, 1910.

Folding painted goose and peacock feather fan. Bone sticks, China, n.d.

Folding peacock feather fan. Stained mother-of-pearl sticks. Paris, 1910.

Folding bleached peacock
feather fan. White
mother–of–pearl sticks.
Paris, 1910.

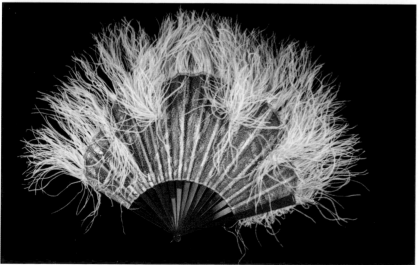

Folding knotted ostrich
feather and lace fan.
Imitation tortoiseshell
galalith sticks. Paris, 1930.

Folding knotted ostrich
feather and lamé fan.
Imitation blond horn
galalith sticks. Paris, 1930.

Folding dyed ostrich feather fan. Mother-of-pearl sticks. Paris, 1930.

Folding natural ostrich feather fan. Brown tortoiseshell sticks. Paris, 1930.

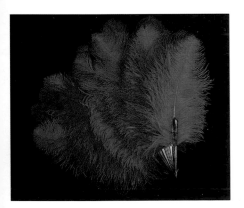

Folding dyed ostrich feather fan. Galalith sticks. Paris, 1930.

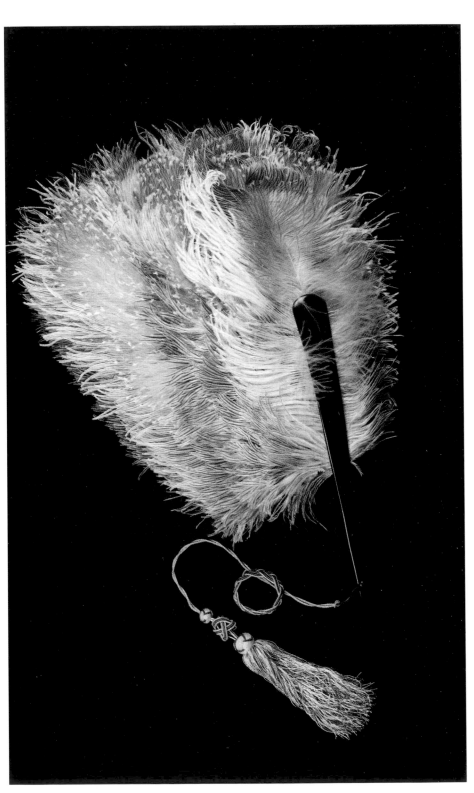

Folding dyed goose feather fan. Red mother-of-pearl sticcks. Paris, 1910.

Folding jay feather fan. Dyed mother-of-pearl sticks. France, 1910.

Reconstituted duck fan. Galalith sticks. Paris, 1910.

Reconstituted jay fan. Galalith sticks. Paris, 1910.

Lace Fans

Cherubs and flowers. Black Chantilly lace on silk. Ivory sticks with monogrammed guard. France, 1890-1895.

Belgium was the principal purveyor of lace used by fan makers during the nineteenth century. Black and white were often associated in obvious symbolism. The Paris fan house Duvelleroy created "Night and Day" models where white lace leaves were sewn on black tulle. Needlepoint lace was readily adapted to the size and shape prerequisites of fan leaves. This however was not the case for bobbin lace. These straight pieces of lace hence had to be assembled to accomodate the curved shape of the leaf by a "joiner" who sewed the lengths together. Lace was popular throughout the century, as it was assimilated to Spanish fashion trends promoted by historical and fictional figures like Empress Eugenie of Montijo and Carmen.

Honiton lace. Pierced ivory sticks. France, 1890-1895.

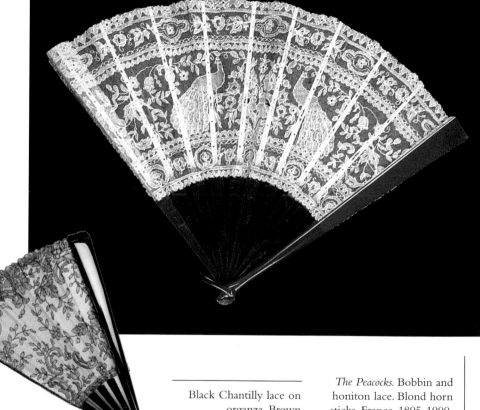

Following page:
Venetian bobbin lace. Blond tortoiseshell sticks. France, 1890–1895.

Black Chantilly lace on organza. Brown tortoiseshell sticks. France, 1860.

The Peacocks. Bobbin and honiton lace. Blond horn sticks. France, 1895-1900.

Duchesse lace. Mother-of-pearl sticks. France, 1890–1900.

Iris. Emboidered tulle with appliqué duchesse lace. Brown tortoiseshell sticks. France, 1890–1900.

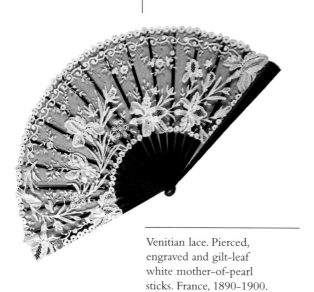

Venitian lace. Pierced, engraved and gilt-leaf white mother-of-pearl sticks. France, 1890–1900.

Venitian lace. Pierced, engraved and gilt-leaf burgau mother-of-pearl sticks. France, 1890–1900.

Sultane fan. Needle point lace. Pierced, engraved and bronzed blond horn sticks. France, 1895–1900.

The Seaside. Brussels needlepoint lace. Pierced, engraved and carved ivory sticks. Duvelleroy, Paris, *ca.* 1870.

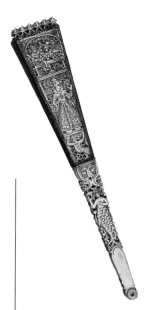

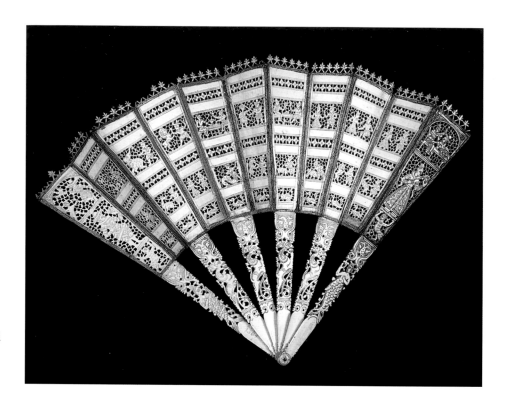

The Hunt. Pierced and engraved ivory folding *brisé* fan. Paper *monture.* Portuguese India, 17th-18th centuries.

Joy. Dance card. Cardboard *brisé* fan. France, 1825-1830.

Pierced Fans

First used during the sixteenth century, the technique of pierced ivory has become synymous with fans and the brilliant skill of the specialized craftsmen, *tabletiers,* who practised it. A single pierced fan guard easily contained more than two thousand holes. The process began with a small saw used to cut the initial openings and generally define contours. The French port of Dieppe was an ivory center and many workshops in the nearby Oise region produced objects in mother-of-pearl, tortoiseshell, bone and horn. One nineteenth century *tabletier,* Désiré Fleury, was renowned for his detailed work with more than two hundred fifty-six holes per square centimeter. Since the beginning of the century, Parisian craftsmen had been using tools with serrated or scalloped edges; punches and dies were used to work horn. The Gothic revival influenced fan makers who sought pierced models with fretwork in the style of flamboyant Gothic cathedrals.

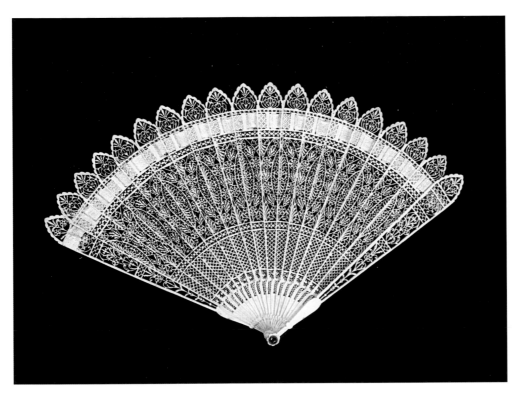

Cathedral. Pierced ivory
brisé fan. Silk ribbon.
France,
1815–1820.

Cockade. Pierced and
engraved ivory *brisé* fan.
China, *ca.* 1810.

Field flowers. Pierced and
painted wood *brisé* fan.
Silk ribbon. France or
Austria, 1870–1880.

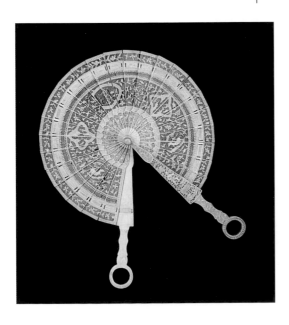

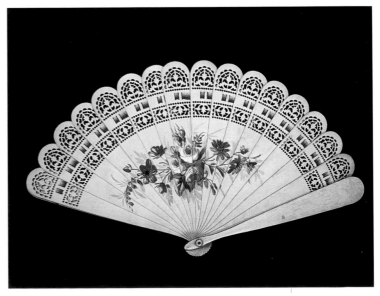

Flower Bough. Gilt-leaf marbled tortoiseshell *brisé* fan. France, 1885.

Top:
Violets. Pierced and painted bakelite *brisé* fan. Silk ribbon. Germany, 1905-1910.
Bottom:
Roses. Miniature painted bone *brisé* fan. France, 1910-1915.

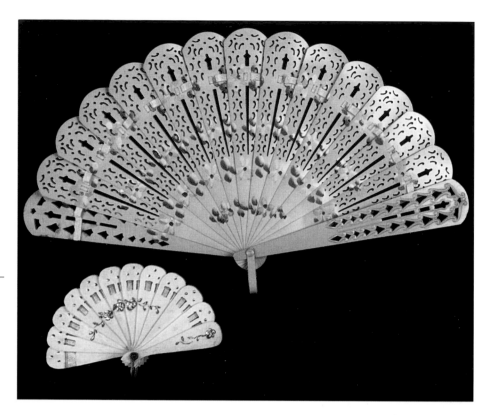

Medieval style. Pierced blond horn and copper *brisé* fan. France, 1815-1820.

Pierced bone brisé fan. China, late 19th century.

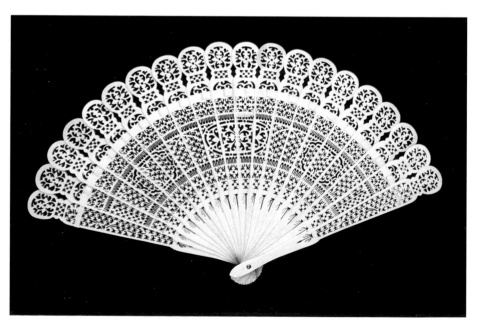

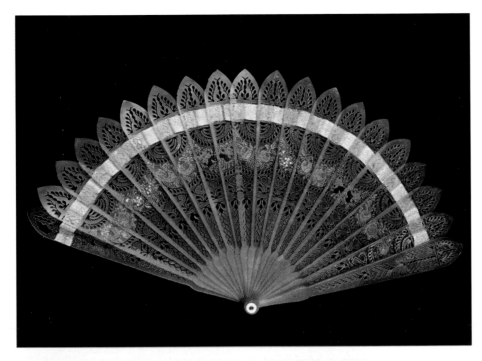

Flower festoons.
Pierced and painted horn
brisé fan. Silk ribbon.
France, 1815–1820.

Brown tortoiseshell *brisé*
fan. Hervé Hoguet,
Sainte-Geneviève, 1964.

Empire sequins. Pierced
blond horn *brisé* fan with
inlaid sequins. Cotton
ribbon. France,
1815–1820.

Fontange. Pierced blond
horn *brisé* fan. Silk
ribbon. Austria, *ca.* 1890.

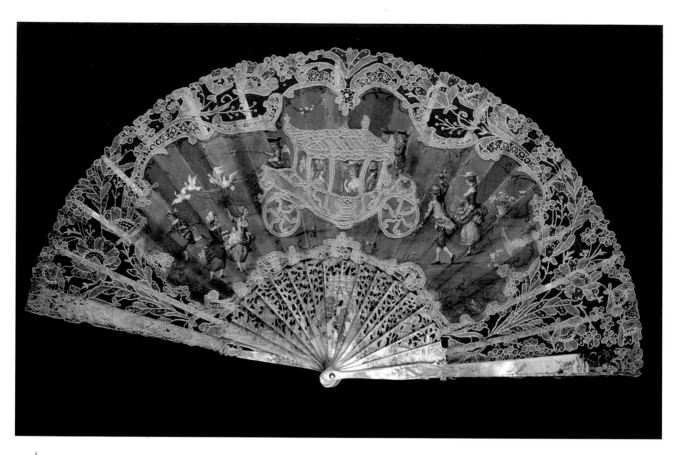

The Carriage. Organza painted by Lasselaz with appliqué honiton lace. Pierced and engraved mother-of-pearl sticks. France, 1900.

Golden Sequins. Embroidered and sequined silk taffeta with appliqué tulle and lace. Engraved tortoiseshell sticks. France, 1910.

Sunflowers. Embroidered silk gauze with silk and gold thread. Galalith sticks with inlaid sequins. France, 1920-1925.

Embroidered Fans

Embroidered fan leaves used a wide variety of materials from common straw to more precious silk thread. The best examples using silk were produced over a relatively short period of time during the 1890's. Floral motifs dominated. Different stitches were used for the leaves and the petals corresponding to different ways of combining colors. For leaves, color zones were clearly defined whereas for petals threads of different colors were juxtaposed. The center of flowers were rendered by a series of knots. Lunéville stitching, a commonly used sewing stitch, was used to secure beads. Embroidered fans remained popular throughout the beginning of the twentieth century and the last ones were produced in the 1920's. Production was however always limited, due more to their fragility than their cost.

Lily of the Valley. Embroidered organza. Ebony sticks. France, 1880-1885.

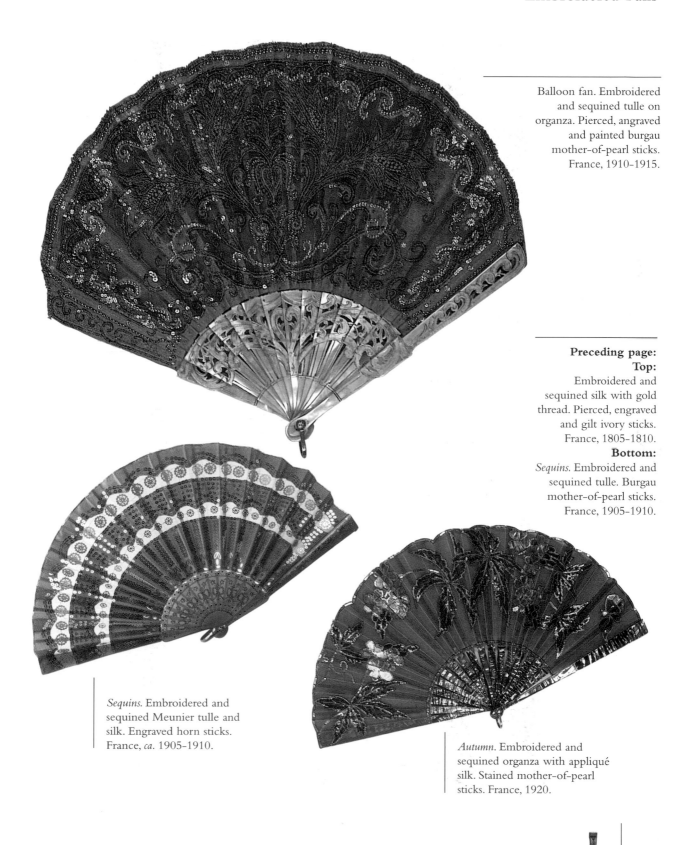

Balloon fan. Embroidered and sequined tulle on organza. Pierced, angraved and painted burgau mother-of-pearl sticks. France, 1910-1915.

Preceding page:
Top:
Embroidered and sequined silk with gold thread. Pierced, engraved and gilt ivory sticks. France, 1805-1810.
Bottom:
Sequins. Embroidered and sequined tulle. Burgau mother-of-pearl sticks. France, 1905-1910.

Sequins. Embroidered and sequined Meunier tulle and silk. Engraved horn sticks. France, *ca.* 1905-1910.

Autumn. Embroidered and sequined organza with appliqué silk. Stained mother-of-pearl sticks. France, 1920.

Art Deco Fans

Sequined organza with appliqué silk. Stained wood sticks. E. Kees, Paris, 1925.

Apart from the enormous human losses of World War I, fans can also be considered as one of its victims. In her quest for equality of the sexes, the liberated *garçonne* of the Roaring Twenties began neglecting fans. Elegance was measured in cigarette holders and pearl sautoirs. Fans were nevertheless still very present for grand occasions. Small ones accompanied dancers while larger models were abandoned on chairs. Advertising introduced them to an ever-growing public. The treatment of flowers and silhouettes was delicate and airy, almost intangible like a soft breeze, while remaining spirited and bold like a dance. And at the end of the decade, fans were quite literally blown away by the Wall Street Crash in 1929.

Painted and embroidered silk fan. Stained bone sticks. E. Kees, Paris, 1925.

Fan designs.
Gouache on paper.
E. Kees, Paris
1920-1925.

Monogram. Bead
embroidered silk gauze
with silver thread.
Galalith sticks. E. Kees,
Paris, 1905–1910.

The Peacock. Meunier tulle
with sequins. Stained
goldfich mother-of-pearl
sticks. France, 1920.

The Pheasant. Painted and
embroidered tulle with
sequins. Galalith sticks.
France, 1910.

The Peacock. Embroidered and sequined taffeta screen with steel beads. Galalith handle. France, 1925-1930.

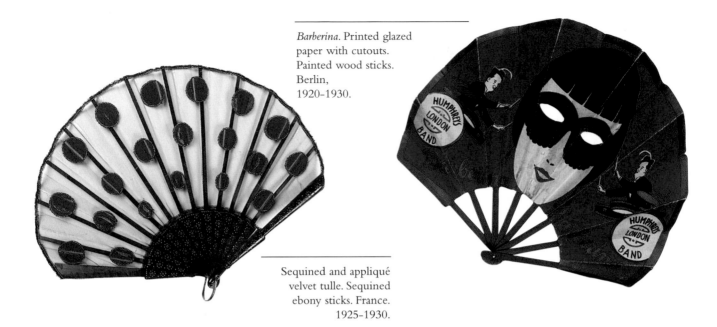

Barberina. Printed glazed
paper with cutouts.
Painted wood sticks.
Berlin,
1920–1930.

Sequined and appliqué
velvet tulle. Sequined
ebony sticks. France.
1925–1930.

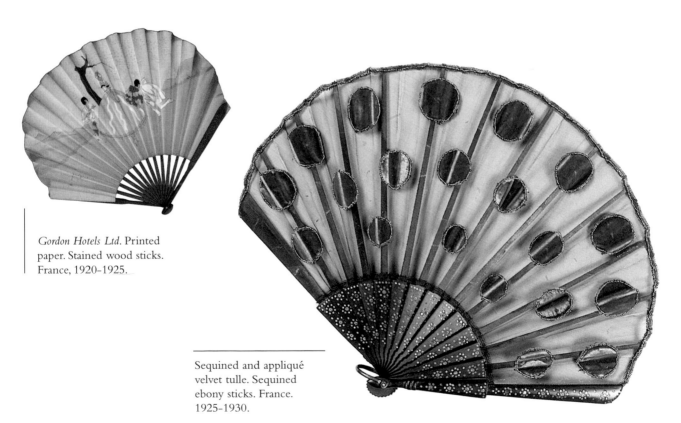

Gordon Hotels Ltd. Printed
paper. Stained wood sticks.
France, 1920-1925.

Sequined and appliqué
velvet tulle. Sequined
ebony sticks. France.
1925–1930.

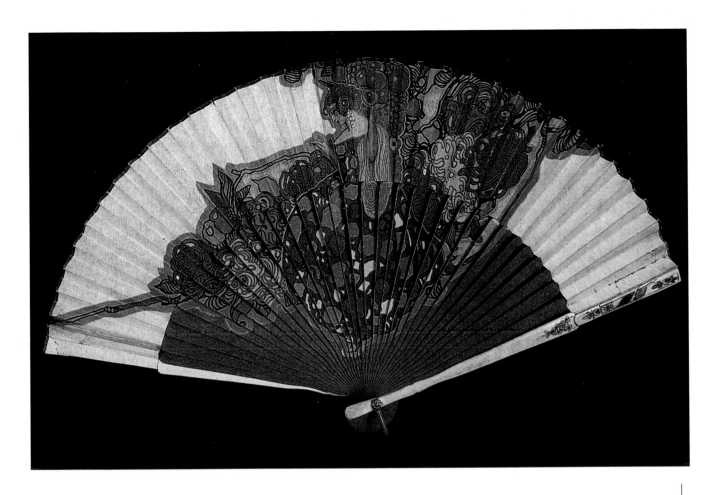

Woman with fruit. Printed paper and wood. Spain, early 20th century.

Bouquet. Painted and embroidered silk. Silk ribbon. Stained bone sticks. E. Kees, Paris, 1925.

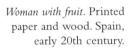

79

Lieutard Orangeade. Cockade. Printed glazed paper. Wood sticks. France, 1930.

Advertising Fans

Advertising fans accompanied the middle class evolution of society. Starting in the late eighteenth century under the reign of Louis XVI, fans chronicled current events in various fields: the first flight of hot air balloons, the taking of the Bastille, patriotic songs to the glory of the Revolution, or the silhouettes of the Royal family concealed in the foliage of a weeping willow. Fans thus had a patriotic role to play, recounting the deeds of illustrious inventors and liberators. They took sides in national and international political debates. Trade guilds commissioned fans to represent and communicate their activities. The passage from social illustration to commercial advertising was a quite natural one, considering the incredible progress in production methods, the ever-widening availability of printing presses — inseparable with the French Revolution, and finally with the invention of show windows, Ali Baba's caverns of consumerism. Fans sold to visitors at the Great Exhibitions of 1889 and 1900 were souvenirs showing the brand new Eiffel Tower and the Alexander III Bridge, a proud testimony to the Franco-Russian Alliance. Restaurants, hotels, wine and spirits merchants and candy manufacturers were prime clients for fan makers. Artists' works confered a lasting elegance to advertising fans. The fashionably thin, long-necked, wide-eyed women depicted by George Barbier appeared on Galeries Lafayette department store fans. These fans were for the most part small folding, ten to twelve stick models between four and eight inches high, printed on colored paper. Some were reminiscent of childrens' book illustrations. On one Bon Marché department store fan, the seven capital sins are illustrated through childrens' games. Absentmindedness has replaced lust.

Le Tribunal de La Haye. Printed paper after Ogé. Wood sticks. Chambrelent, Paris, 1930.

Pernod 45. Printed paper.
Wood sticks. Buffault,
Paris, 1925–1930.

Amer-picon. Printed paper after
Rochegrasse. Wood sticks.
France, 1925–1930.

Cherry Rocher. Printed
paper. Wood sticks.
Chambrelent, Paris, 1929.

Pikina. Printed paper.
Wood sticks. France,
1925–1930.

Amer Picon, recto and
verso. Cockade. Printed
paper. Wood sticks.
France, 1930.

Florio, le meilleur Marsala,
recto and verso. Cockade.
Printed paper. Wood
sticks. France, 1930.

Confiserie Lamy. Cockade.
Printed paper. Wood
sticks. France, 1940.

Chocolat Poulain. Cockade.
Printed paper. Wood
sticks. France, 1930.

Pernod export. Printed
paper. Wood sticks.
Chambrelent,
Paris, 1930.

Chocolat Lombard, recto
and verso. Printed paper.
Wood sticks.
Chambrelent, Paris, n.d.

Cointreau and Vouvray, closed
and opened. Cockade. Printed
tissue paper. Wood sticks.
France, ca. 1900.

Au Bon Marché, recto and
verso. Painted paper.
Painted wood sticks.
France, 1925.

Au Bon Marché. Painted
paper. Painted wood
sticks. Japon, s.d.

Au Bon Marché. Printed
paper after A. Lopez.
Wood sticks. J. Ganné,
Paris, 1925.

Au Bon Marché. Printed
paper after A. Lopez.
Wood sticks. J. Ganné,
Paris, 1925.

Au Bon Marché. Painted
paper. Bamboo sticks.
France, s.d.

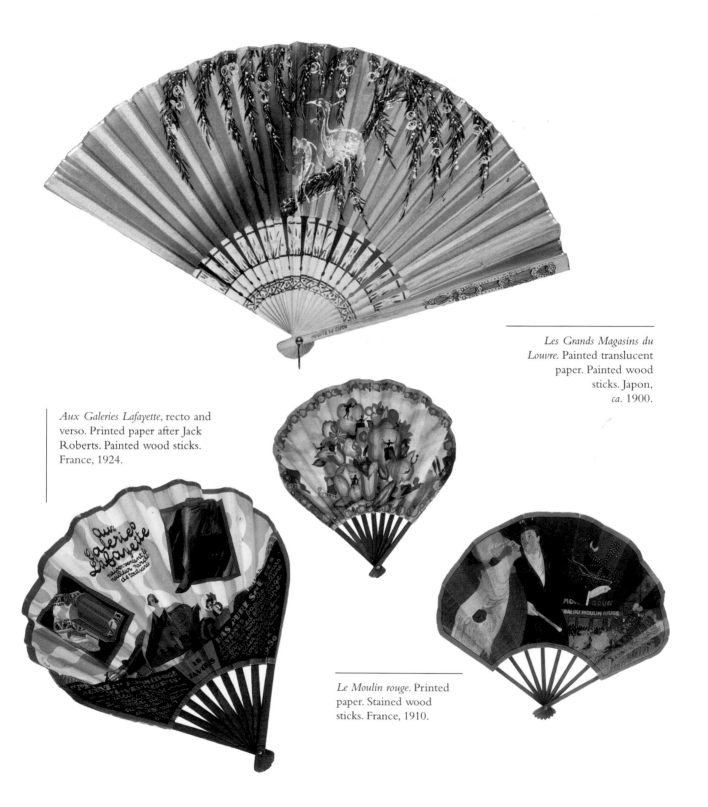

Les Grands Magasins du Louvre. Painted translucent paper. Painted wood sticks. Japon, *ca.* 1900.

Aux Galeries Lafayette, recto and verso. Printed paper after Jack Roberts. Painted wood sticks. France, 1924.

Le Moulin rouge. Printed paper. Stained wood sticks. France, 1910.

Vichy Hôtel, recto and verso. Printed paper. Stained wood sticks. France, 1925.

Palmette fan. Painted and sequined crêpe paper. Wood sticks. Carnaval Novelty Co. Ltd, London, *ca*. 1910.

Chromo paper palmette fan. Painted wood sticks. France, late 19th century.

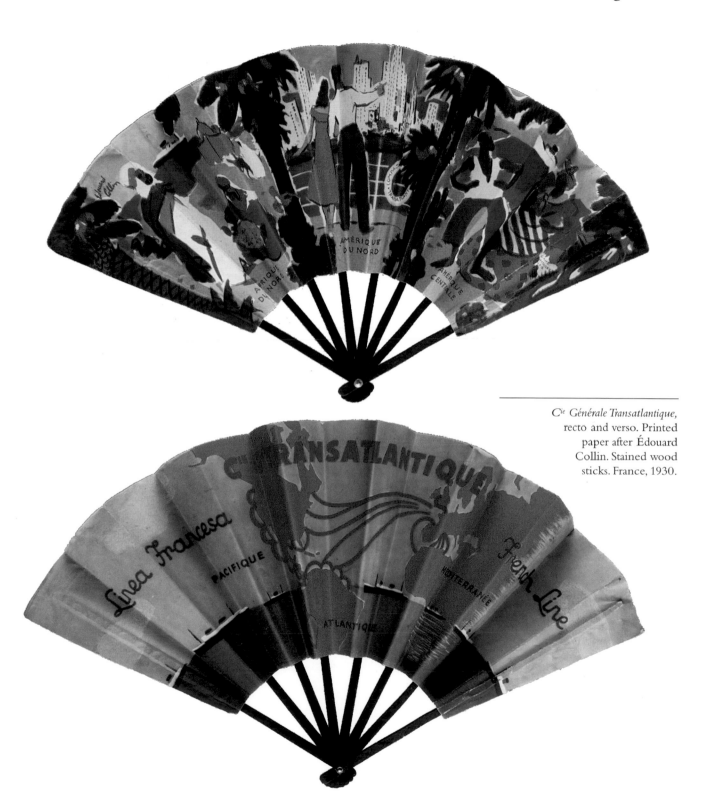

Cie Générale Transatlantique, recto and verso. Printed paper after Édouard Collin. Stained wood sticks. France, 1930.

Humorous Fans

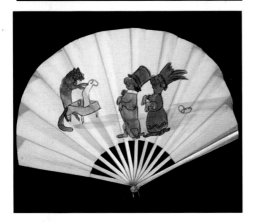

Lithography contributed to the transformation of popular fans as leaves were no longer decorated by artists but by draftsmen. What better way than a fan to share an amusing image ? Gavarni, however, was an exception and continued in his role of social commentator. Line became liberated, more daring. Fans began to occupy an intermediate place between posters and illustrated newspapers. Hotels and restaurants, sports, bars and cafés, ideal clients for humorous fans, offered them to selected patrons. The French caricaturist Francisque Poulbot left a memorable *Café de la Paix*. Unfortunately, these mass-produced articles announced the beginning of the end for fans.

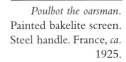

Poulbot the oarsman. Painted bakelite screen. Steel handle. France, *ca.* 1925.

Circus, designs by Jova. Paint and chalk on vellum paper. Bone sticks. E. Kees, Paris, 1900-1910.

See Saw.
Chromolithography on
paper. Wood sticks.
France,
1940–1950.

Nursery Rhyme.
Chromolithography by
Oto on paper. Wood
sticks. France,
1940–1950.

Novelty Fans

The first fan with mechanism dates most probably from eighteenth-century France under Louis XVI . Edouard Petit, who had improved the leaf mold, also perfected the slide fan. Throughout the second half of the nineteenth century, innumerable patents were issued and their secrets jealously protected. André, Baron, Clochez, Ducrot, Garam, Maillet: all these unsung inventors attempted to pass along to posterity new and improved models. For example, Ducrot's sun screen popped out of its case at the push of a button. Generally, the models reflected the society that engendered them, one where people met at the theater or on promenades, hence looking-glass and lorgnette fans as well as parasol and umbrella fans. While the ventilator fan is supremely logical, others like the key or the handkerchief fan were more or less practical.

Left:
Collapsible tube fan.
Cherry wood and printed
fabric. France, 1920-1930.

Right:
Ricordo. Cockade with
mirror. Spain, 1870-1880.

 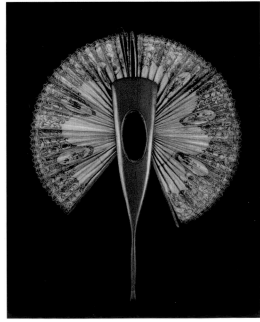

Key fan. Painted papier mâché. Painted paper cockade. J.-B. Bonnard, *ca.* 1900.

Carved horn brisé fan. Hervé Hoguet, Sainte-Geneviève, 1964.

Folding pocket fan monture. Galalith and metal studs. France, 1890.

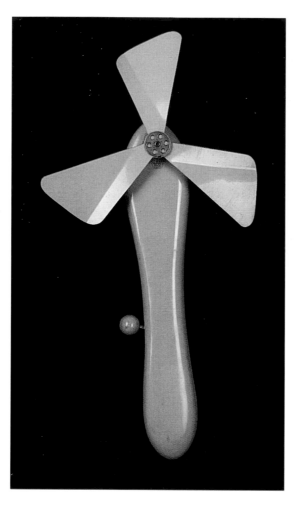
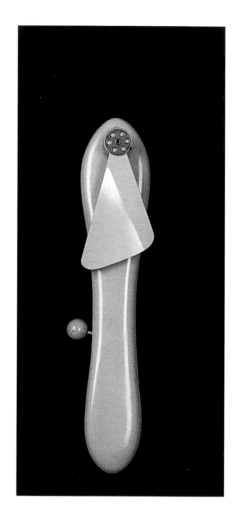

The Zéphir. Rhodoid and bakelite pocket fan. The Zéphir et Cie, Paris, 1901.

Painted silk folding pocket fan. Bone sticks. France, *ca.* 1855.

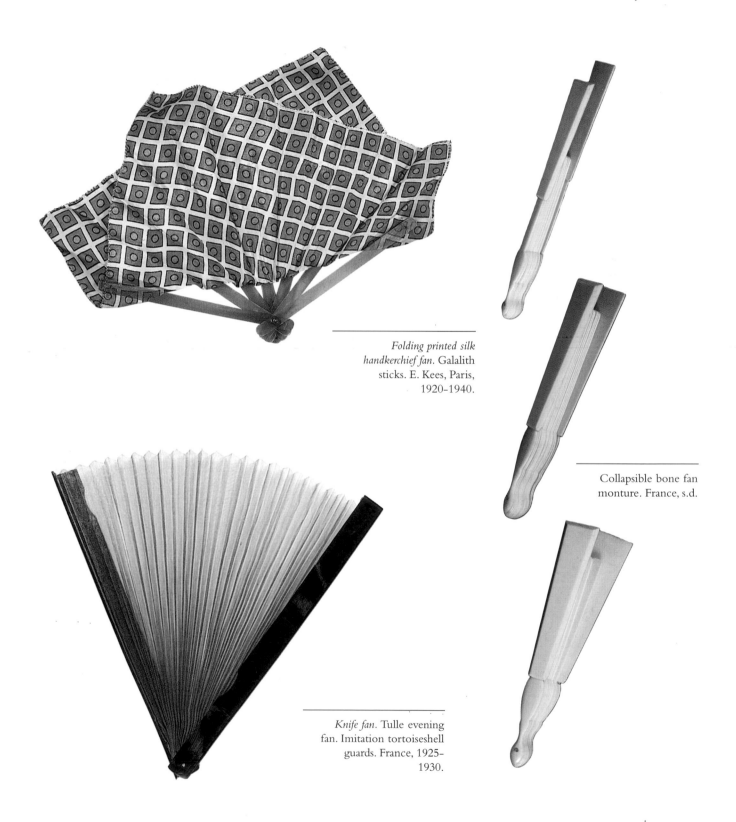

Folding printed silk handkerchief fan. Galalith sticks. E. Kees, Paris, 1920–1940.

Collapsible bone fan monture. France, s.d.

Knife fan. Tulle evening fan. Imitation tortoiseshell guards. France, 1925–1930.

93

Bibliography

Perthuis (F.) de. *Éventails*, Paris, 1989.

Volet (M.). *Éventails européens*, Musée d'Art et d'histoire, Geneva, 1994.

Soussa (J.) de. *La Mémoire lithographique*, Paris, 1998.

Les Éventails du XVIIIᵉ à nos jours, Museum of Chateauroux, 1996.

Deberne (H.-J.). *Danser en société*, Paris, 1999.

Bonnet (L.). *Tabletterie, le bouton, l'éventail*, 1998.

Bouvot (C. et M.). *Dentelles normandes*, Condé-sur-Noireau, 1997.

Villani (E.). *Sulle Ventagli del Tempo*, Milan, 1999.

Das Gewisse Etwas der Riez des Fachers, Historical Museum, St Galen, 1991.

The Fan Museum
2, boulevard de Strasbourg
75009 Paris
Tel : 01 42 08 90 20

Open to the public on Mondays, Tuesdays and Wednesdays (except for national holidays) from 2 p.m. to 6 p.m.

Premier Fan museum in France sharing premises with the Anne Hoguet studio, master fan maker.

Three centuries of fan history presented in the 1870 showroom of a fan maker on the Grands Boulevards in Paris.

In 1872 Joseph Hoguet established his workshop of fan frames at Saint Geneviève in the Oise, renowned center of *tabletiers*. His son, Hervé, continued in his footsteps. In 1960, he acquired the Ernest Kees house stock of antique fans, then moved his workshop to Paris and the premises of the Lepault and Deberghe house in the traditional fan area. The museum's revolving collection is in fact presented in their 1870 showroom (in the process of classification on the supplementary list of Historical Monuments).

Today Anne Hoguet continues the family tradition. She forms students and directs production and repairs in the workshop which is open to museum visitors.

Photoengraving: Édilog, Paris

Printed in April 2001
in Italy

Dépôt légal 2e trimestre 2001